TRUMP'S BATTLE AGAINST THE FAKE MEDIA

****

DOES THE FAKE MEDIA CARE ABOUT THE TRUTH ANYMORE?

ANSWER: IT SEEMS AS THOUGH THEY DO NOT. HOWEVER, THROUGH OUR OWN EFFORTS WE AS CONCERNED AMERICANS MUST BRING THE FAKE MEDIA BACK AROUND TO BEING WHAT IT IS SUPPOSE TO BE; OR DISPEL THEM.

TRUMP'S BATTLE
AGAINST
THE FAKE MEDIA

****

SHOULD HE WIN? YES!!!

WILL HE WIN? YES!!!

PRESIDENT DONALD JOHN TRUMP IS THE FIRST AMERICAN "PRESIDENT" TO CHALLENGE THE FAKE MEDIA IN THE MANNER THAT HE HAS------

SHOULD HE BE SUCCESSFUL? YES!!!

AN IN-DEPTH AND HONEST LOOK AT THE FAKE MEDIA AND THEIR UNSUBSTAINTIATED BATTLE AGAINST PRESIDENT DONALD JOHN TRUMP AND THE CURRENT WHITE HOUSE---------

THERE IS VERY GOOD NEWS IN THIS BOOK;
PLEASE READ!!!!!!!!!

Acknowledgments

I just want to thank all my friends, my family and supporters who gave their honest feedback on the different drafts of the manuscript, which immensely helped me out to polish all the information. And to thank all those people who inspired me, contributed to my knowledge, influenced me, and assisted me in the creation of this guide – I thank you all from the bottom of my heart!

Table of Contents

Introduction, Overview, and What This Book Entails:

THIS BOOK IS A MUST READ!!! DO NOT WRONGFULLY JUDGE OR PASS JUDGMENT ON ANOTHER POLITICIAN, AMERICAN CITIZEN, OR PERSON UNTIL YOU HAVE READ THIS BOOK!!! THIS BOOK CONTAINS SOME VERY STRONG TRUTHS ABOUT THE AMERICAN SOCIETY: A SOCIETY THAT WE ARE SO FORTUNATE TO BE ABLE TO BE A PART OF!!! AMERICA AND ALL ITS LEADERS, POLITICIANS, AND CITIZENS MUST ADHERE TO THE IDEALS CONTAINED IN THIS BOOK; OR WE ARE HEADED FOR A FALL!!! AS AMERICANS, WE NEED HELP!!! THERE IS VERY GOOD NEWS IN THIS BOOK!!! PLEASE READ AND COMPREHEND; IF YOU CAN!!!

AS YOU READ THIS BOOK, REMEMBER THIS: RULES AND LAWS PROTECT US ALL!!!

This book is about truth, the righteous path, the greater-good, and what GOD ultimately wants for this great nation called "America." Also, this book is about those who want to support the above whether they are Black, White, Hispanic or any other race. However, this book is not about religion; but rather about structure, the rule of law, fair-play, and justice. Again, this book is definitely NOT about religion. However, there is VERY GOOD NEWS in this book!!!

Further, this book exposes the deep-seeded spiritual conscientiousness that we all as human-beings are born with; which should encompass our government structure, our politics, and our laws. Simply put, we all innately know the difference between right and wrong and justice vs. injustice.

There are certain behaviors that must be indoctrinated into a society and within a nation for that nation to be able to function successfully and to be at peace internally among the citizens. Citizens of any nation must have Laws, Rules, and Regulations for the people of that nation to be able to function properly and to have harmony, peace, and for justice to prevail among them.

A nation also must have some basic principles to be able to create and retain order and fair-play within a nation. I think America's core principles that are deeply rooted in our laws and within the US Constitution stem directly from the Bible and are the principals that have made us the greatest and most powerful nation on the earth. Americans strive to have a GOD-conscientiousness about themselves; and our laws, rules, and regulations stem from those biblical principles. The point is, American law reflects that we as Americans try to be a fair and just people.

Thus, because of this, this is a nation that is blessed by GOD. GOD and JESUS believe in Justice, Fair-Play, Order, Structure, and a righteous alignment in all aspects of life, and more-so within the Government. Romans 13 clearly states "obey the government, for GOD is the one that put it there." And it further states, "So those who refuse to obey the laws of the land are refusing to obey GOD, and punishment will follow."

Therefore, when certain citizens of a nation CLEARLY do not follow the rules of that nation, they should not be able to participate in the fundamental privileges of that nation and/or be penalized and/or be marginalized in some manner. This is especially true when holding political leadership positions and when it comes to FAKE media reporters. This is the only way that people can thrive in a society and feel that they are being treated fairly and will be treated fairly.

This is the core theme and message of this book. With that being said, it does not matter whether you are black, white, brown, yellow or any other race or color. Further, it does not matter whether a citizen calls themselves Republican, Democrat, Independent, Conservative, Liberal, Moderate, Progressive or whether you are far-left or far-right. Also, it does not matter what religion you affiliate with. In other words, feel free to identify yourself as you wish, but play by the rule of law, which should be applied the same across the board to ALL people. Another way to put it, justice "should" be blind.

Frankly and personally, I think it is best to identify oneself as an independent because one has the flexibility to be able to support good candidates, to be able to support the truth, and to be able to support what is just-and-right on a case-by-case and on-going basis without being locked into any one type of political party or position. In other words, the independent has the flexibility, to be able to support that which is for the greater-good for the society and for the Country within either party, on a case-by-case basis.

However, the main point is this, when people are not willing to abide by and obey the laws and rules set by a society, then they should be marginalized in some manner to keep the fabric of justice and fair-play in-tact. Many democrats and some anti-trump protesters have resorted to very low and illegal tactics from the time that Hillary Clinton lost the race for the Presidency. They have resorted to lying, mayhem, destruction of property, riots, obstruction-of-justice, and violence against Trump supporters.

When people are allowed to get away with these acts it degenerates the system of government and the society becomes down-trodden and FAITHLESS. Further, it is just morally wrong. What happen to peaceful protest?

The above actions are the very reasons why many voters have rejected most of the Democratic Party in this particular era in politics. The Democratic Parties' ratings have not been as low as they are now since the 1920's. Many Democrats have exhibited behaviors that are extremely immature; they have tried to cheat in the democratic process; they do not want to follow the rules or laws unless it benefits them; they create untruths about other politicians to distort and confuse the citizens; they try to race-bait; they play the race card; they are involved in the obstruction-of-justice; and they do not honor the American system when things do not go their way. So very immature.

Basically, most of them who act this way are acting like spoiled little children who did not get their way. Crying, sniffling, and pouting for reasons that are out of their control. Boo-Whoo! These particular democrats and citizens really have no business trying to acquire leadership positions in America and this is exactly why they are starting to be rejected by the voting citizens of America. Good for us! So very good for us!

By the way, there are some Democrats that are not fooled by the fake media and are not creating lies about the President and do put the love of our country first. This should be the big picture for all of us. To put what is best for the Country first and foremost.

This book is not to expose or bash any one particular person, or a particular party or group; necessarily. However, this book's core objective is to expose UNTRUTH; IMMATURITY; EXTREME BIAS; BLACK RACISM; WHITE RACISM; RACISM; UNFAIRNESS; HATRED; JEALOUSY; and CONSPIRACY to distort the truth all along the political spectrum; among the media; and from any citizens. So therefore, we must let the chips fall where they may.

This book is written for all those who seek the best for America, those who seek what is right in the eyesight of GOD, and for those who love Justice and fair play. It is specifically written to call-out those who are trying to deceive the American people and gain leadership by trying to wrongfully bend the rules in their favor and create false narratives to keep their inconsistent and false agendas alive. No one is above the law. No one should try to construe the rules.

Therefore, let's play by the rules and by the law. If you choose not to, then you need to be exposed, penalized, and expelled from the political arena; and/or marginalized as appropriate under the circumstances; until you have come back to your senses. It's just that simple.

DONALD JOHN TRUMP

T his book is also, in-part, dedicated to the Great American Citizen, Donald John Trump, for his insight, for his foresight, his strong will, his courage, and his undaunted high energy to make America Great Again. From the onset, Donald J. Trump's attempt to seek the Presidency of the United States of America has been a major challenge for him and quite a spectacle for most Americans to see. Many did not, and could not see his unique talents coming to the national political scene. Starting with the highest ranking Republican Party members, all the way down to the lowest Democratic members, few could tell that Donald Trump was a rising star on the National Political scene; and most wrote him off as a joke.

Nevertheless, through all of the fake media press, the unfair and biased debate commentators, the lying Republican rhetoric during the campaign, and through many people who did their best to discredit Donald Trump; he still won and is now in-fact the United States President of America. Thank GOD!

It takes a strong willed person to accomplish what Trump has accomplished in the face of these odds. Further, it shows that he really wanted the position and that his heart was really into becoming President.

Trump, in-fact, started working and doing things that a President is supposed to do even before he was elected; whenever he got an opportunity. For example, he met with the President of Mexico; amongst other endeavors.

Trump ran a high energy campaign. Every morning when he woke up, the only thing that was on his mind was defeating anyone who stood in his way to becoming the next US president; including defeating Hillary Clinton and her massive campaign machine and money.

Donald Trump spent way less money than Hillary Clinton on his campaign, and he further tried to campaign in accordance with truth and facts. While on the other hand, Hillary Clinton used negative campaign ads and lies to try to destroy Trump's chances. Further, Hillary used her money machine to deceive many Americans to believe that she was the better of the two for the White House. She created many false narratives about Donald Trump through her campaign ads and other devices.

However, for Hillary, it didn't work. Americans saw through her lies and deceit and her relentless unscrupulous attempt to push her way into the White House. But again, it didn't work. Thank GOD!

Her biggest mistake, which she probably realizes by now, is using her private instruments to conduct classified and top-secret government business on an ongoing basis knowing that it was illegal, unethical, against the rules, and wrong. Further, and what is just as bad, is that she committed perjury and continues to lie about the wrong doings.

Additionally, President Obama tried to convince voters that Trump was racist and a supporter of the KKK. Even President Obama and his fantastic swagger and dynamic oratorical political voice could not dismay Trump believers. Hillary Clinton also brought in famous Black celebrities such as the famous rapper Jay-Z and famous music icon Beyoncé to help her campaign and to try to curve the Black vote in her favor. Yet still, it did not work.

THE DILEMMA

Donald J. Trump won the Electoral College 306 to 232 fair and square and by playing by the rules. What is further damaging about this is: Even though Donald Trump won the United States Presidency fair and square, many, especially many democrats and some other weak fragile leaders will not have the decent common courtesy to at least honor the fact that he is the new duly elected President. They will not acknowledge the fact that he won the office fair and square. President Trump has even reached-out to embrace Democrats and other Trump opposers during his acceptance speech and on other occasions; and most Democrats and Trump opposers have "CONSTANTLY" rejected him for no legitimate reasons. What is he suppose to do? This is very sad and immature!

First, they say Trump cheated by fixing the vote count. Not true. Then they say the Russians affected the vote count outcome. Not true. Then they say Trump colluded with the Russians. Not proven true. Then, they say he should not win because he did not win the popular vote. Irrelevant and unfounded. Now they say he is a supporter of White Supremacy, Neo Nazis, and the KKK. Totally untrue and unfounded. Now they are also starting a rumor that Trump has an on-set of a medical condition called dementia; that he is unhinged; and suggesting that somehow he is not in-touch with reality or is somehow demented or delusional. So much unsubstantiated nonsense, immaturity, and pettiness!

Now, Hillary Clinton has released a book trying to tarnish President Trump as a person and as the recognized President of America. Further, the fake media and some democrats scrutinize every word he says and they constantly look for anything that they can use against him. They give him no credit for anything; even if he says exactly what they want him to say, or do exactly what they want him to do. So sad and so immature! And, they continue to make up any news story to discredit his victory and his reign as the President. Utterly ridiculous and childish!!! Such immature cry-babies!!!

Even further, some Democrats, and many Black Democrats did not attend his inauguration. Many Black Democrats are using racism as a scape-goat rather than face the truth and be honest and honor Donald Trump as our new President. Many Black Democrats call him racist with no proof or evidence. Some Blacks will not refer to him as President or acknowledge the fact that he is the President. Some say, including Black civil rights leader John Lewis, "He is not a 'legitimate' President." I am a Black American myself, and I say this is so Immature and childish, and they should ALL be ashamed of themselves and grow-up. And some of them should not be holding any office. And I am sure that John Lewis and other Black people's late Idol and spiritual leader, Dr. Martin Luther King Jr., would not approve of this immature, irresponsible, and utterly divisive behavior. These actions have no merit. These actions hurt our country as a whole and these people are not putting the best interest of the country first.

Some Black Democrats, such as Maxine Waters and Al Green, have called for President Trump's impeachment and are still calling for his impeachment without proper protocol and procedure, proof, or evidences. Anything Trump says is construed in a negative light or twisted into a falsehood or untruth by many Black Democrats, Black Leaders, regular Democrats, Trump haters, and the fake media. In their petty minute view, nothing that Trump does is good enough for them; again, even when he does exactly what they want him to do or say. And again, President

Trump has reached-out to embrace Democrats and other Trump opposers during his acceptance speech and on many other occasions, and most Democrats and Trump opposers have constantly rejected him. They exhibit such hatred and jealousy against Trump without due cause. Once again, such childishness!

It is really so funny that some people can always tell President Trump what he ought to do and say, but they do not do the basic things that they should do and say as basic human-beings and as American Citizens; such as showing basic human-decency; such as accepting the fact that Trump is in-fact now the duly elected President; and giving him basic respect as a human-being; and also as the President of the United states. Some of them literally act as though he is suppose to obey their every "whim." Again, so ridiculous!

We all know that no one is perfect and that we all make mistakes. However, these immature Politicians, Reporters, and people never have anything nice to say, or never give Trump credit WHEN CREDIT IS DUE. They act as though they themselves are perfect. They act as though Trump is suppose to "dance" to their every tune and obey everything that they tell him to say or do; and yet they do not give him the common courtesy or common respect that every human-being deserves (especially since he is the President). So utterly ridiculous, immature, petty, and so very unfair! These types of people will not win in American life, as a professional, or in American politics exhibiting these kinds of unfair behaviors.

All of these childish Democrats, childish Republicans, childish news reporters, childish Blacks, childish Whites, childish leaders, and childish politicians need to be excommunicated from participating in the roles that they are in because they are not playing by the rules or by the law; and they are not exhibiting the notions of fair-play, honesty, and justice. To be quite frank, those who act in this manner are acting like a bunch of cry-babies and are acting very immature like spoiled little children.

Democrats, Republicans, Politicians, and News Reporters who act this way have no place in public life, no business holding public office, no business holding any professional position or leadership role, or no business reporting the news; because once again, they are not honoring and playing by the rules and putting the interest of the Country first. They are holding the Great Nation of America back from being all that it can and should be! They should be happy that we True Americans are actually carrying them and tolerating them while they are in their disillusioned state of being; until they come back to their senses and reality.

Again, this is exactly why they are being rejected by the American voters. And again, these actions hurt our country as a whole and these people are not putting the best interest of the country first.

THE FAKE MEDIA

For the fake media who are also participating in this destroy-President-Trump-campaign; they too should be marginalized and excommunicated from reporting the news. The news is about reporting the truth and facts in an objective manner. It is not about putting a favorable spin on the news to suit any particular person or party's needs or wants. It is not about trying to destroy or discredit someone like they are doing the President. These News Reporters truly should be ashamed of themselves and should suffer some sort of reprimand or some serious penalties, as appropriate.

The Fake Media is a Big Problem in our American society. It could be argued that the Fake Media is the "biggest problem" in our society because it permeates many, if not all, aspects of our lives. Fake media has the potential to be destructive in all facets of our American life.

When people are not getting the truth or the facts, they are making decisions and operating in their daily lives based on false and inaccurate information. They cannot truly make proper and accurate decisions because they do not have proper and accurate facts and truth in which to base their decisions upon. Thus, they are making decisions based on false premises, and therefore they cannot make adequate and appropriate decisions because of such fake news. Many lives have been destroyed, cut-short, or limited because of Fake News. This is so very unfair in our society and we must fight against this utter distain upon the American society in every way we can; because this should not be so.

"PRESIDENT" DONALD JOHN TRUMP

I think we have one of the best Citizens in America as our new President – Donald J. Trump. He was certainly the best choice out of the two choices, by far! Trump is eager to make America great again by doing what he feels is necessary to get the job done. He is very high energy at the age of 71. He works very hard and relentlessly every day to fulfill his campaign promises. He is consistent in what he says and does.

"President" Trump is the first American "President" to challenge the Fake Media in the manner that he has. The Fake Media CERTAINLY needs to be challenged by a high office such as this because the Fake Media has been ruining lives in America for many years.

Thus, this book serves, in-part, as a tribute and a salute to President Trump's service as a great American trying to do the will of the American people; and the will of GOD.

Therefore, we support President Trump and his fight to dismantle the fake media and those who oppose the advancement of American democracy; and this book further exposes those negative people and entities.

Please keep reading and enjoy, while we try to give an insightful & honest analysis & look at this political crisis & dilemma! Again, please enjoy!

Chapter 1:

Trump Upsets the Media by Becoming US President

Donald Trump, the renowned American businessman, is now the president of the United States, having succeeded President Obama and taken office in January 2017. Trump's win was a surprise to a section of Americans, especially because it is rare for a serious presidential candidate to emerge from ordinary citizens who have never held a political office before. Nevertheless, the biggest shock was experienced by the media, particularly the mainstream media that was clearly anti-Trump from the very beginning. They could not believe that this successful businessman who did not care to be in good books with them ended up winning, beating his main rival, Hillary Clinton, who was media's favorite.

Trump's Fame before Politics

Trump is not new to the media. For many years, he has run a TV show, *The Apprentice*, which has had high ratings and exposed him to the public limelight in a big way. To the businessmen and women he was trying to groom on the show, Trump was a straight shooter; never mincing words when he thought someone was terrible at their job. He became famously known for his statement: *You are fired!* Despite media's prejudices against Trump, many Americans have not forgotten the admirable side of Trump they had seen from the show. They had witnessed firsthand his ability to make bold decisions even when those decisions were not necessarily popular. This is a side of Trump that many Americans liked, because they felt the country needed someone who was capable of making bold decisions that favored the citizens, even if those decisions upset some people or even some countries.

It is for this reason that Americans proceeded to elect Trump president, even when the media kept up the hype about how bad it was for Trump to speak of stringent immigration laws and deportation of illegal immigrants. In fact, the media wanted it to appear as if Trump was going to indiscriminately deport everyone who was not a US citizen, even when that was not the case. To their disappointment, a good number of people from the same affected communities ended up voting for Trump and that helped him win against Hillary Clinton. The communities with the most immigrants, including the Hispanics, could see that the media was biased in favor of Clinton and prejudiced against Trump, and that they did not necessarily have their interest at heart.

Media Houses Were Unabashedly Anti-Trump

Many of the big media houses were outright against Trump. During the presidential campaigns, *The Washington Post*, for instance, outright accused Trump of continuously flip flopping on the issue of immigration. Yet he was bold enough to respond to media questions. One wonders why the media does not frame their questions in a manner to get clarity instead of making up sensational stories. However, such behavior is not surprising when the media house has another candidate as their favorite – in this case, Hillary Clinton.

As for The New York Times, they alleged that the way Trump intended to handle the issue of immigration shows he takes immigrants to be criminals. They proceeded to say that such criminalization was an attitude of the '80s that should not have a place in the current America. The truth is there was no time that Trump said or implied that all non-US citizens are criminals. Instead, he kept explaining that the security of the country is paramount, and it is important that everyone in the country be legally accounted for if US citizens are to be effectively protected. Often the media bashed Trump only because he was frank. When illegal immigrants commit crimes, it is a fact that it is much more difficult to catch up with them than it is to follow up and nab a US citizen, or a resident who is in the US legally.

As for CNN, it expressed its anti-Trump views, alleging that he was trying to antagonize Americans by talking tough on immigration, yet the US is no longer attractive to natives of South America. According to CNN, South Americans, of course including Mexicans, had lost their wish to come to the US since the US economy dipped in 2007. As far as the media house was concerned, the South American economies had greatly improved and their population growth fallen, so the people that Trump thought were dying to flock into the US were not interested. That argument was not based on facts if you look at statistics provided by the Pew Research Center. In short, the media house just wanted to discredit Trump's position on immigration, irrespective of the fact that security is a sensitive issue to everyone residing in the country.

NBC's bias for Hillary Clinton as compared to Donald Trump was clear in its reporting. When the Hillary Clinton's e-mail scandal was at its peak, the media house downplayed it, yet when a section of the public staged protests against Trump, the media house was very enthusiastic in reporting about them and replaying the images on TV.

Media Tried To Cause Split within the GOP

Trump maintained the same spirit he manifested in The Apprentice, of telling it as it is, as he conducted his presidential campaign. This straightforwardness first became clear during the party primaries, when Trump competed against 16 candidates under the Republican Party. Each of the other candidates had served either as Senator or Congressman in the US at some time or the other, unlike Trump who never held a political office before. As the media drummed it into Americans the disadvantage of running for the highest office on the land without having prior experience either as Senator or Congressman, Trump focused on explaining to the citizenry the need to have a president who was not beholden to the Wall Street moguls, and who would not be slowed down by bureaucracy.

Trump may have failed to win over the media, but he, definitely, won the hearts of the Republicans. Ultimately, he became the GOP candidate to run against the Democratic candidate, Hillary Clinton. It is ridiculous how, even then, the media still tried to split the Republican Party, insisting the party should not allow Trump to be their flag bearer. Luckily, the US is a country that follows rules, and the GOP could not afford to be seen to be changing its rules for the sole reason of locking Donald Trump out of presidential contention. In any case, he had already won strong followers among the conservatives, and soon some of his party rivals rallied behind him – people like Chris Christie, New Jersey Governor, who had vied for party nomination alongside Trump.

Media prejudice against Donald Trump was not a general feeling but reality that had been ascertained by professionals. A Rasmussen Report, for instance, released in May 2016, indicated that 49% of people likely to vote in the presidential elections saw media as having been prejudiced against Donald Trump. In comparison, a similar report of a survey done 6mths before – December 2015 – had the percentage of people with the same sentiments as 47%. In short, with each passing campaign day, the media was becoming increasingly anti-Trump. Whereas a TV channel like Fox was sometimes seen as toning down any prejudice against Trump, the Rasmussen Report still showed that only 18% of potential voters saw the media as being prejudiced against Hillary, in the May report, the proportion having dropped from 24%, which was the December percentage. Rasmussen Reports is a respected American company that deals with public opinion polling.

The Hypocrisy of Some Conservative Preachers

All through the presidential campaigns and after, there were some conservative Christians who saw Trump as not worthy of being associated with the conservative party. The GOP has traditionally held conservative principles, mainly based on Christianity, and some of its supporters judged Trump's image of an outgoing flamboyant rich man as not a good match. Some even criticized Trump's choice of televangelist Paula White to say a prayer during his inauguration, simply because they felt she is not conservative enough. Like Trump, White has divorced twice, has filed for some bankruptcies over time, and she is a proponent of people trying to become wealthy – what the conservative Christians dub prosperity gospel.

The reality is that those who have criticized Trump for pursuing riches through his business endeavors, and White for preaching God's power to make people rich, do not necessarily live humble lives. As such, one cannot fail to see their hypocrisy, even when veiled under the guise of conservatism. On the other hand, Trump understands that it is only when people are motivated to create wealth that the country can prosper. That is why in his presidential campaigns he was proud to expound on his business prowess and good business judgment. It looks like although Trump's outlook to wealth is self-explanatory, conservative Christians keep deliberately misinterpreting it just to make him look bad. For Christians who are supposed to love one another, these conservatives are blatantly hypocritical, especially considering the deep dislike they seem to have against Evangelicals like Paula White.

Chapter 2:

Reasons I Support President Donald Trump

To put it bluntly and in a nut-shell, the reasons why I supported and voted for Donald Trump are as follows: Donald Trump was the most mature and the most Presidential among the Republicans and Hillary Clinton, he believes in Law and Order (which we really need in this era), he is not the traditional Politician, he is a successful business-man and knows how to get things done and how to get people to do things, he speaks from the heart and is true to his current and past convictions, he educated us as Americans about current politics, he will try to build the wall on the Mexican Border to keep America Safe and keep the criminal element out, he wants to put American ways and norms first and foremost, he wants to make the English Language first and foremost (not Spanish or some other foreign language), he wants foreigners to assimilate to us as Americans (not us assimilate to them), he is not a racist, Trump will enforce the borders in accordance with current law, he will probably be good at dealing with ISIS and any kind of threat or terrorism towards the US from foreign countries and otherwise, he seemed to be having fun while running for President, he is a very smart man and has very strong convictions, and he has a good heart.

Also, Trump will be wise when it comes to foreign affairs, national policies, and being Commander-in-chief; and lastly, I support

Trump because we need a LION in the white house to deal with the evils that face America, especially in foreign affairs. Donald Trump is that LION who will protect American interest and will fight terrorism and other perceived evils. In addition, people who have fun at their job seem to do a better job. President Trump seems to be having fun being President and enjoys the challenges that it entails.

Donald Trump is here to stay, and I believe he is the right president for the US right now. Not only has the US been threatened by terrorism and economic problems, it is also true that the country has lost much of its clout as an international power. President Trump is the leader who can help the country become more prepared to protect itself against home grown and international terrorism, and also to improve its economic well-being. He is the one person who has what it takes to make the US an influential super power again.

This is, of course, not the message the US mainstream media is sending to its citizens. On the contrary, they keep portraying White House as a disorganized place and a place of scandals. It is like they want to justify the reason they said negative things about Trump during the presidential campaigns. The negative publicity notwithstanding, Donald Trump remains the most mature of the presidential candidates the GOP provided in 2016. And that is one of the reasons I support him.

Trump believes in law and order, and he will not let people mismanage the affairs of the country whether they are his friends or not. He illustrated this during the presidential campaign period, when he relieved some of his charges of their duty and replaced them with others he believed were more efficient. For instance, he sacked his then campaign manager, Corey Lewandowski, just before the GOP convention. President Trump is not the traditional politician. He just wants things done and does not care about retaining friendships at the expense of achieving his goals. This is very important as president because often presidents fail to fulfill their campaign promises owing to the inadequacies of their political lieutenants. Trump may appear to enjoy being in the limelight, but his drive to succeed will not let him work with people who cannot perform.

Trump's Business Success Proves He is a Doer

Donald Trump has been a successful businessman for many years, and considering the cut-throat competition there is in business, being a billionaire means he is well versed in economic matters, a good manager, and a shrewd decision maker. It is clear the reason he ran for office as president was to implement the moves he believes need to be made in order for the US economy to shine, and for Americans to have better quality of life. Anybody questioning Trump's ability to improve the country's economy needs to look at the business empire he built as an ordinary citizen.

He has golf courses across the world, including in Muslim dominated areas. He has golf courses in the United Kingdom, Dubai, and in different states in the US, including Florida, New Jersey and North Carolina. He also has luxurious hotels all over. These hotels have not only earned him lots of revenues, but they have also been America's pride. So, when Trump speaks of making America great, he wants to empower every American to be part of that effort. And from his personal experience as a citizen, he knows this is possible. Now that he is in power, he is prepared to work towards eliminating the bottlenecks that previous governments have put in place, which deter individuals from succeeding in business.

He Can Improve US Security

Luckily, many Americans voted Trump in as president because they admired the way he spoke from the heart. They could relate to what he said and liked his convictions. Even when he spoke of building a border between the US and Mexico, it is for the benefit of Americans. Nobody can dispute that the porous US/Mexican border poses a threat to Americans because of the drugs that come into the country from Mexico. Consequently, no logical person can dispute that criminal elements are able to come into the country through the same border, thus endangering the lives of US citizens. Why the media and other Hillary Clinton supporter's cannot see this is beyond understanding. Clearly, they are blinded by their prejudice against Trump.

He Prioritizes US Interests

Whereas many US citizens would love to see the country back to where it used to be on the global arena, influencing world politics and economics, few past presidents have had the valor to take action towards that direction. In the process, the US has continued to be overshadowed in economic power and political influence. President Trump wants to change all that by making the US known by everyone globally as the country to pay attention to, when it expresses its stand on issues. During his campaign, he spoke of withdrawing from organizations that do not benefit the US, and he has begun taking action in that regard.

Trump has, for instance, given formal notice to the UN, expressing US intention to withdraw from the Paris agreement. This agreement, which seeks to have countries drastically bring down the level of greenhouse gas emission, is unfavorable for the US. It would cost the US a massive number of jobs, yet the US does not cause as much pollution as other countries within the same umbrella of the Paris agreement; countries such as China. One thing that makes Trump admirable is his go-getter attitude, and ability to circumvent bottlenecks. For example, the exit clause in the Paris agreement demands that a member country waits for 4yrs before expressing its intention to withdraw. However, Trump has found a way of circumventing that bottleneck and is about to relieve the US of obligations that are unfavorable for the citizens.

As for the Trans-Pacific Partnership (TPP), it is the first alliance he sought to withdraw from once he took office. In fact, he did this through an executive order. He could not see how the US was going to benefit from being confined in a group of 12 countries, some of them struggling economies, just because they share a common border – the Pacific coastline. During his presidential campaign he always spoke of preferring bilateral trade agreements, and in this case he prefers to negotiate with countries like Japan and Singapore, or its immediate neighbor, Canada, instead of working with them as part of the TPP. His idea is to enter agreements that are beneficial to the US, and not to remain in organizations simply to endear himself to the world as a team player.

In addition, president Trump has the terrorist organization called ISIS on the run; a terrorist organization that Hillary Clinton and President Obama are at least part of the major reason why it could form and take root, could sprout, could grow, and could blossom. She and Obamas poor foreign affairs policies and skills helped to create the terrorist organization known as ISIS.

He Wants To Reinstate American Pride

Trump wants English to take priority in the US, and not Spanish or any of the other languages spoken mainly by immigrants. He passionately wants foreigners to make the effort to assimilate in the

American culture, as opposed to expecting Americans to adapt to their ways. This is in no way racist, but an attitude of national pride. The media was on the forefront during campaigns to portray Trump as racist, but this is an allegation that does not hold water. For one, Donald Trump is married to an immigrant, his wife, Melania being a Serbian by birth. Besides, when he speaks of tightening the law on immigration, it is in a bid to protect US residents from incoming criminal elements. He actually has no problem with immigrants who have processed their US residency legally the way Melania did. Melania worked as a fashion model in the US but took the initiative to take up permanent residence in 2001, and US citizenship later in 2006.

Chapter 3:

Why I Did Not Support Hillary Clinton

To put it bluntly and in a nut-shell, the reasons why I did not support or vote for Hillary Clinton are as follows: Hillary Clinton has lied and committed perjury before congress and under subpoena, she has destroyed evidence while under subpoena before congress, she has jeopardized the safety of America by miss-handling classified and top-secret information, her maid was exposed to classified information, she is not trustworthy, she is a proven liar and deceiver, she has participated in the Obstruction of Justice, she wanted open borders (BAD IDEA), and she is a grave danger to the safety, the security, and the sanctity of this nation.

Further, Hillary Clinton is messy and deceitful and could not run a clean campaign about the policies and American issues (she had to slang mud and nasty gossip), she has not shown the type of qualities that a President should show, Bill Clinton has been accused of rape and sexual assault by many females (Trump has not), Bill Clinton's Attorney license was revoked, Hillary does not play by the rules, she does not follow the law, she is a liar and tries to cover up her lies until exposed (very bad trait), she destroyed evidence (cell phones and computer servers) after a subpoena was given by congress (which is the obstruction of justice and it also shows that she was hiding something because she knows she was guilty), she destroyed thousands of emails (evidence) even though the emails were under subpoena by congress (again, obstruction of justice), and she used her office as secretary of state as a bully pull-pit for her own personal gain and wealth for the Clinton Foundation.

And once again, Hillary Clinton and President Obama are at least part of the major reason why a terrorist organization such as ISIS could form and take root, could sprout, could grow, and could blossom. She and Obamas poor foreign affairs policies and skills help to create the terrorist organization known as ISIS.

Further reasons why I did not support or vote for Hillary Clinton are as follows: I believe Hillary Clinton uses people for what she wants and does not have any sincere benefits to offer to our National Office as president, she only wants to be president to say she is/was the first woman president and for the power and recognition that it entails, and she only caters to Black Americans to get the black vote.

I really do not believe that she believes that she can really solve or assist in truly solving some of the Black issues that we as Black Americans face. Further, she referred to young black Americans as Super-Predators, she called over half of the population of Americans irredeemable and deplorables (only GOD should judge people in this manner), and she was only using President Obama to get what she wanted (the Black vote).

Further, Hillary Clinton has a bad relationship with the politicians in congress and other politicians because of the lying, the obstruction of justice, and perjury; she probably would not get any bills passed through congress or get anything done because her relationship with congress is not good.

Hillary Clinton's aides had to plead the 5th amendment because of her directing them to commit criminal or wrongful activities. Our country is spinning out of control and Hillary has no Law and Order skills, Hillary Clinton's character traits to be the leader of the highest office in the land are far from acceptable, she has had innocent people killed with her foreign policy decisions, she is not fit to be President and does not have a proven track record, and lastly we need a LION in the white house to protect American interest. Hillary Clinton is not a LION, she is too passive, and she lacks the judgement and the temperament to be commander-in-chief.

Based on the above, having someone like her in the most prestigious office in the world, after all that has been proven that she has done, is definitely NOT the right message for our country and for our children. Having Hillary Clinton as President would have definitely had a negative impact on the righteousness and the Justice that our Country is known to stand for and to be about. Further, and most damning, with her having committed the acts above, she surely does not legally qualify for any Federal Office and certainly not for the Presidency of the United States of America.

Also, if both candidates were evil, and I had to choose the lesser of two evils, Donald Trump is certainly head-and-shoulders a better choice than Hillary Clinton. Donald Trump is not a Saint, but he certainly is not a criminal and he does try to play by the rules.

Hillary may be a smooth talker, but she is not the best person for president. In fact, compared to Trump, Clinton is no match. There is a lot of bad judgment that one can cite from her long history in the political arena, first as senator for New York and then as Secretary of State. Even as first lady during the presidency of President Bill Clinton, she still manifested poor judgment.

Hillary Often Lies

Hillary Clinton is, clearly, economical with the truth on personal matters as well as matters of national importance. In October 2016, for instance, she alleged that James Comey, then FBI Director, sent a set of her e-mails that were subject of investigation to only Republican members of Congress. According to the FBI director, this was not the case, and he had not sent the e-mails in a selective manner. At some point it was even said she had destroyed some e-mails and phone records that would have confirmed she had compromised US security during her tenure as Secretary of State.

Hillary Clinton lied to Congress under oath, and there was even an outcry for her to be sued for perjury. Parts of her response to questions posed during her testimony regarding her use of her private server for official communication was contradicted by the evidence produced by Comey, the FBI director. If Clinton had been a straightforward person, she would have provided all the e-mails demanded by the investigating team, and then either apologized to the country for her recklessness, or defended her decision to use a private server for official communication.

She Endangered National Security

By destroying crucial evidence when the investigation on her use of her personal server was going on, she was clearly making it difficult for security organs to determine how best to improve national security, especially in relation to high ranking government officials. It is also shows that she has little respect for the law, since even courts rely on evidence to determine cases. It makes you wonder if she would be interested in strengthening the independence and efficiency of federal courts.

When it comes to the issue of Benghazi where the US lost a number of soldiers and diplomats, Clinton lied to the bereaved families as well as the general public that the Benghazi attack was a result of Muslim outrage, following a video posted online by an Egyptian Coptic Christian, Nakoula Basseley Nakoula. As it turned out, the so-called inflammatory material was not the trigger for the attack on US embassy in Benghazi. Worse still is the fact that Hillary Clinton knew the truth all along. From an e-mail she sent her daughter soon after the attack, it was discovered she attributed the Benghazi attack to Al Qaeda, the infamous terrorist organization, formerly led by Bin Laden.

And once again, Hillary Clinton and President Obama are at least part of the major reason why a terrorist organization such as ISIS could form and take root, could sprout, could grow, and could blossom. She and Obamas poor foreign affairs policies and skills help to create the terrorist organization known as ISIS.

She Lacks Personal Integrity

When President Bill Clinton, Hillary Clinton's husband, was accused of sexual harassment by some women, Hillary went on an all-out attack, portraying her husband's accusers as cheats and individuals eager to get some limelight. Even when it was finally clear that Bill Clinton was a philanderer, Hillary Clinton did not apologize to the women she had portrayed in bad light. Such a person would not be expected to entrench personal liberties, let alone advance women protection. In fact, considering no such ugly accusations were ever made against Donald Trump, he is a better person to protect women than Hillary Clinton.

Looking at Donald Trump's history, it is clear he is interested in women empowerment from the many he has employed, and the many that hold senior positions in his organizations. On the contrary, Hillary Clinton is not known to have assisted women improve themselves even when she has been well placed to help them. Instead, she did not only bash those who accused her husband of making sexual advances; she was also known to relate poorly with women working in White House during her husband's presidency and those working under her.

Her Ambition Is For Personal Gain

Hillary Clinton's ambition to become US president is out of a will to occupy the highest office in the land; to hold the most prestigious office. Were it not true, she would be having a lot to show for the time she has been US senator and Secretary of State, or even from the time she practiced law. Unlike Donald Trump who came to vie for presidency with a long list of achievements in his business field, there is no significant mark in the legal profession or in the political arena that can be attributed to Hillary Clinton. Apparently, her main drive was to go down on record as having been the first woman to hold the most prestigious political office. In short, Hillary Clinton's self-serving ambition, as opposed to Trump's that is geared towards making the US a wealthy respected nation.

She Is Not Convincing

Hillary Clinton lacks authenticity, unlike Donald Trump whose convictions are easily transmitted to his audience. She lacks charisma, and as such it would be difficult for her to put Americans at ease where serious issues of security and the economy are concerned. The media has tried to say good things about her, emphasizing the experience she has had in matters of politics, but on the bit that only she can do, which is portraying herself as a credible leader, she has failed. She does not attract undivided attention once on the platform, and when she speaks she does not seem to speak deep down from the heart like Trump. Yet, in order to have the country rallying behind you as president, it is important that the people feel your conviction. Further, she spent much more money towards the campaign than Trump did. While Trump's entire spending was impressively only $600 million, Clinton ended up with an expense of $1.2 billion, yet, she still could not thwart the support from the people that Trump was getting.

Even with the bias the media has had, it has been difficult for them to lie about some things like Hillary's charisma. At some point, *The Guardian* noted how she lacked authenticity and charisma, and they pinpointed the fact that it is difficult to unite the nation with those two qualities missing. Even the *Daily Beast*, wondered how Clinton expected to win votes when she had minimal charisma. It looks like poll numbers were being manipulated to suit Hillary Clinton, and this is clear from sentiments expressed through platforms away from mainstream media. For instance, once Reddit users wondered how Clinton remained in the lead when she had so little charisma. Now that Donald Trump is president of the US, it is easy to look back and admit that Hillary was never really in the lead during the campaigns, but was being portrayed as such by biased media.

She Has Poor Judgment and bad temperament

Hillary Clinton's poor judgment was a talking point during the 2016 presidential campaign. Even her Democrat rival, Bernie Sanders criticized the poor judgment she manifested by voting to invade Iraq in 2002.

People close to Hillary Clinton know her to have a bad temperament, and that is very different from being a strong leader.

One secret service agent, Gary Byrne, who worked close to Hillary Clinton when Bill Clinton was president, terms her as erratic and sometimes violent. He has written a book and in it he terms Hillary Clinton's leadership style as volcanic. He describes her as impulsive, and one who has the tendency to create sycophants. Needless to say, sycophancy can easily compromise the security of the country even as it kills the morale of sincere hardworking officers.

These dangerous traits that Hillary portrays cannot be associated with Donald Trump, because whereas Trump expects his team to be loyal to him, he is prepared to listen to their opinions. It is, therefore, easy for Trump to make decisions on the basis of the reality on the ground, whether these decisions affect the economy, national security, or any other sphere. If Hillary were president, other politicians, diplomats and employees would, very likely, be scared of volunteering information and expressing their sincere opinions, thus leaving Clinton to make decisions that may affect the country adversely.

Chapter 4:

Why Blacks Should Support Trump

Midway through the 2016 campaigns, a good number of Black Americans realized that Trump was their best bet for presidency. In any case, they had not witnessed Hillary Clinton pushing their agenda in the various positions she had held before. Yet they had seen Donald Trump give equal opportunity to Blacks through his famed reality show, *The Apprentice*. True, there were some Blacks who were carried away by the anti-Trump media hype, but the ones that supported him did so with conviction and passion. On the whole, it is easy to understand why the Blacks who supported Trump did so, and I fully concur with them.

Some of the well-known Blacks who openly supported Trump included former apprentice, Omarosa Manigault and Dr. Ben Carson who also ran for GOP presidential nomination. Omarosa Manigault actually served as Director of Trump's African-American Outreach during the campaign period. Mike Tyson, former World Heavyweight Boxing Champion, also supported Trump, saying he is the only person of such caliber who has shown respect for him as a person. Stacy Dash, a host on Fox TV channel, also supported Trump, just as Dennis Rodman who has his own vodka brand to his name. Together, they provided important points for supporting Donald Trump, even as the media continued to portray him as racist.

Trump Wants To Give Blacks Opportunities

People who want to live a life of dignity cannot be happy living on food stamps all through their life. That is why President Trump intends to create economic opportunities for every US citizen, American Blacks included. He also intends on pushing for opportunities that favor Blacks as a marginalized group; such as making it easy for disadvantaged African-Americans to access soft loans, which they can utilize in business and repay slowly. African-Americans accessing such loans would be able to initiate business ventures, and this can be the beginning of a successful business career for those who work hard and are focused.

Also, the fact that Trump plans on having some unfavorable taxation laws reviewed is a testament to his determination to make doing business convenient and rewarding. One of the nagging regulations he intends to have reviewed in order to make it easy for hardworking Americans to do business is the so-called Dodd Frank act. Many Blacks have been unable to sustain their businesses, even when they have the entrepreneurial spirit, simply because the cost of doing business has been high, and the mesh of complicated regulations puts them off. With Trump geared towards making it conducive to do business, I see why more and more Blacks are rooting for him.

However, even with such glaring facts, the media does not seem prepared to highlight the positive side of President Trump. They would like it to appear that the Black community has all along been anti-Trump and still are. They ignore the fact that many Blacks openly declared their support for Trump during the campaigns, and they continue to show support even now that he is president. It is also ridiculous how the media ignores the fact that Donald Trump garnered more votes from Black voters than Mitt

Romney did back in 2002 when he vied for the presidency under the same Republican ticket.

Blacks Should Remember Past Media Lynching

The fake news is nothing new. The fake news has been around for many years, but it is about time they are called out by someone like President Trump to expose their ill-will. Please allow us to lay out our case.

As the media tries to sway Black-Americans and African-Americans in the way they perceive President Trump, it is good to recall how fellow Blacks have fallen victim to media lynching themselves, just as has been happening to Trump. In short, it would do the Blacks a lot of good to take biased media reporting on Trump with a pinch of salt.

If the media was sincere about wishing to see the lives of Black Americans improved, they would be contributing ideas for President Trump to consider, or giving helpful ideas to various members of Congress for favorable legislation to be passed. This is, however, not happening, and all the media is interested in is bashing President Trump on scandals that allegedly took place during the 2016 campaigns.

It behooves every Black-American and African-American to remember the unfair treatment various Black personalities have received from the US media. One pitiable case was the one where the late pop singer, Michael Jackson, had been accused of rape by a youngster whose family he had hosted and assisted. The media was quick to convict Michael in the public arena without proper evidences. Another case of the media judging a Black person before being heard is that of O.J. Simpson, who was accused of killing his wife, Nicole Brown. In a televised interview with Greta

Van Susteren in 2004, OJ Simpson said that the media has a major negative impact on our legal system. Minister Louis Farrakhan, a Black American known for his Black activism, has expressed unfair treatment by the media regarding his religious stance. Wesley Snipes has used the term fake news in regards to himself on a YouTube interview. Please see https://www.youtube.com/watch?v=7LPm8F8pSaU. The late Legendary Music Artist, Actor, and Musician, Prince, very seldom gave interviews with the media because he never had any faith or trust in the media. Prince felt that the media would always turn true news accounts into sensational false stories for monetary gain to line their own pockets.

Even Thomas Jefferson, the 3rd US president, though not Black-American, was alive to the fact that the media can be brutally prejudiced against individuals. As such, it is wise that Black Americans judge Donald Trump on merit, evaluating tangible moves that can benefit them and gauging them against real gains received or missed from past regimes.

Chapter 5:

Democrats' Immature Attitude Towards Trump

It is sad that members of the Democratic Party do not seem to have accepted the fact that Donald Trump is president, and that they have no chance of calling the shots for the next four years. They have been manifesting immature behavior particularly in Congress, where they have been doing their utmost to block any legislation or amendments that the Republicans bring forth for debate. The Obama Care that Donald Trump promised the electorate would be scrapped or repealed, has been on the table; and every time the Democrats have been barring any attempts to amend any part of it.

The immaturity becomes clear as the Democrats continue to hinder progress on legislation, yet they do not offer any plausible solutions. They seem to forget that the US is still one nation that needs to move forward in all matters, including those that touch on health. Much as they would like to show that Obama Care has not been as bad as Donald Trump portrayed it, they also need to consider that matters of health care and health insurance are actually matters of life and death. While it may be said, and truly so, that the Republicans also tried to frustrate success of legislation initiated by the Obama administration, the reality is that two wrongs do not make a right, and the American people are increasingly getting frustrated by the Democrats' behavior. They can sense the revulsion many Democrats have for Trump, but that is not helpful to the electorate, be they Whites, Blacks or Hispanics.

Immature Politicians are bad for the US

The behavior the Democrats are exhibiting by frustrating legislation in Congress does not endear them to the general populace. Instead, they are creating an image that makes Americans question whether they wanted Hillary Clinton to rise to power just to keep the Republicans out, and not to do good for the country. In fact, it is likely that such behavior from the Republicans is part of what led the electorate to support a candidate who had no association with the immature attitude exhibited by each of the big parties at one time or the other. If the Democrats continue in this manner, wasting precious time in Congress, President Trump might find himself earning sympathy from Independents and ordinary citizens who are normally supportive of the Democratic Party. Ultimately, the party could find itself greatly weakened come 2020.

What politicians often forget is that their history counts when it matters most. That is why, for instance, Hillary was reminded during the presidential campaigns that she had voted for the baseless invasion of Iraq in 2002. Sadly, as the Democrats in Congress continue to frustrate Trump's progress, the media that should be gunning for the good of the country is silent. Instead, it is focusing its attention on issues that the Democrats are passionate about – those that portray President Trump as being unfit to lead the US.

Media's Unhelpful Obsession with Russia Links

Trump has been forced to refute mainstream media for their obsession with the Russia issue. It has been said that top officials in the Trump administration engaged in talks with officials of the Russian government as US campaigns continued, and that has become a bone of contention with the Democrats alleging that Russia must have interfered with US elections. Of course, the reason Democrats say so is because their candidate, Hillary Clinton, lost the elections, and while such excuses can be understandable, the media is taking it too far. No wonder President Trump has expressed his frustration on twitter for all and sundry to see. He has singled out CNN, MSNBC and NBC for being obsessed with the Russian issue.

The US Media Has Not Duped the US Populace

The media continues to sensationalize Trump's association with Russia, but luckily, Americans are not easily duped. They can see the media bias for what it is and are not swayed to believe that Donald Trump won the presidency unfairly. In fact, the Gallup survey done mid-year indicates that only 24% of ordinary citizens take TV news seriously. So, even in matters of Russia having interfered with the 2016 presidential elections, the general public has not bought into it.

The media did its best to portray Trump as an unfit candidate for presidency during the campaigns, and now that he is the president despite the bad press, they are bent on showing there were underground forces manipulating the 2016 presidential elections. While this may not have any legal consequences against Donald Trump or his presidency, it surely has an impact on the speed at which Trump's efforts bear fruit. For instance, investors might hold on bringing their investments to the US, waiting to see which direction the so-called links-with-Russia takes. As such, jobs that would have been created in a year's time may now take longer.

Chapter 6:

More Credible People Confirm Media Bias

It is often said no single person is an island. Likewise, no one country can survive and thrive in isolation. As such, President Trump has been reaching out to leaders of other countries, with a view of working together for the good of the American people. Other leaders have also reached out to Trump for the same reasons, and because they would like to be in favor with the US president. It is not surprising that other nations would like to get along with President Trump, considering the US is arguably the strongest worldwide in terms of financial and military power, and other countries could do with its support when in need.

Many people who have had a chance to talk with the president have realized he is not as heartless and unreasonable as the media has tried to portray him. In fact, they do not see why anyone should fault another for trying to acquire the best things for his people, which is what Trump has been trying to do for the US.

Media Has Treated Trump the Harshest

In the past, different US presidents have had their share of scandals, some personal and others work related. However, Trump feels that the media has not treated them as unfairly as they have treated him. As he expresses his disappointment, one cannot forget how mainstream media went all out to discredit him during the presidential campaigns, to the extent of inciting former employees to speak ill of him.

Trump also used to hold the US beauty pageant franchise, and during the campaigns the media gave a lot of exposure to beauty pageants who spoke ill of him. One cannot fail to wonder where the media has been all through if they had wanted to assist employees or beauty pageants that Trump had allegedly treated unfairly. The media timing is, obviously, questionable. After all, Trump has been a public figure for many years and his businesses have been done in the open.

Trump tells Youth to ignore Media Distraction

The fact that President Trump is still on course with his work is amazing considering the many distractions the media has been causing. In May 2017, when addressing the congregation at Coast Guard Academy, he advised the fresh graduates of the need to remain focused even when the media behaves the way it does with him. The graduates responded in cheers, meaning they concurred with President Trump on the issue of unfair treatment by the media. He emphasized that the behavior the media criticized him for during the campaign, and the resilience he showed, are the very aspects that made him win the presidency. In short, his stance is that the fact that he won the 2016 elections despite the odds means his principles are good and he is doing things right.

The GOP still has faith in President Trump

Trump's political party, the GOP, still has faith in President Trump, although the media has managed to cause apprehension within a section of legislators. A Michigan legislator, Justin Amash, expressed his fears that the allegations being made against

Trump, particularly the alleged attempt to interfere with investigations, might lead to the president's impeachment. Still, it is important to note that the legislator was responding to a question asked by reporters, and the way the media tailors questions regarding Trump is often subjective and leading. If they want the interviewee to express negative sentiments, they frame the question in a manner to elicit a negative response. The questions are often geared towards provoking answers that do not favor Trump.

Media bias notwithstanding, a good number of legislators who hold key positions in the Republican Party, notably Speaker Paul Ryan, have expressed their confidence in the president despite the many allegations, especially the reports the New York Times and the Washington Post sensationally made regarding the Russia related investigation by former FBI director, Comey. Legislators like Ryan understand that the allegations against Trump are just part of the media lynching that began during the US presidential campaigns. He even told reporters that it was clear some people were out to discredit the president, but the Republican Party could not join the media fray and begin to judge the president when they had not found any facts to back up the allegations.

Even the US Senate has refused to be carried away by the media witch hunt and has not blamed President Trump. Instead, when the mainstream media made a chorus of Trump's attempt to interfere with the investigations related to Russia, the senate decided to do its own investigation. They asked Andrew McCabe, who is the acting chief of the FBI, to submit any relevant documents to the Senate, so that its intelligence committee could see if there was any incriminating evidence against the president.

Not Every Democrat Believes The Media

The media may drum up dislike for President Trump, but not everyone is buying into it – not even his rivals, the Democrats. Newspapers and TV channels have dedicated a lot of space and time respectively on Trump's alleged improprieties, but Americans of integrity have refused to accept some of it.

For instance, when responding to the media, a Democrat Senator from California, Diane Feinstein, stated clearly that it would not be in the US interest to impeach the president. According to her, impeachment should not be considered if there were other options, even if it was found that some allegations against the President had a trace of truth. This is indication that there are still many Americans who care about their country the way Trump does, and would not jeopardize the presidency just to discredit a candidate from a different party. It also shows that not every American swallows everything the media says just because the media is insistent or repetitive.

Fake News Has Been The Trend

Ever since Donald Trump expressed his intention to run for presidency, the media has portrayed him in bad light. That notwithstanding, he proceeded to become the GOP candidate, and later on the President of the United States. Instead of the media acknowledging they were wrong in the way they judged Trump, they have continued to justify their stance by spewing out more and more lies about Trump.

For instance, they have all along portrayed Donald Trump as a candidate who cannot get along with other world leaders, in fact someone whom other world leaders dislike. In spite of that bad press, it has become clear that other world leaders are prepared to work with President Trump. In fact, some of them have spoken out about the prejudice shown by the US media against Trump. For instance, in May 2017, on an interview with GQ Magazine, former UK Prime Minister, Tony Blair, spoke of how unfair the media has been to President Trump. He said the Western media is polarized and partisan, and seems to find it very difficult to be objective about President Trump. Nevertheless, he does not buy into the media allegations and is quick to dismiss them. He even welcomed the idea of Theresa May inviting President Trump to the UK.

Respected World Leaders Have Met With Trump

Tony Blair, who served as British Prime Minister beginning 1997 up to 2007, has visited the White House during Donald Trump's presidency, and this is indication that he respects the president. During his meeting with President Trump's senior advisor, Jared Kushner, Tony Blair expressed dismay at how some people within the Democratic Party seem to be blinded to any good Trump could offer. He termed them too partisan, which is a term he has already used on the Western media. It, therefore, seems like the media has succeeded in brainwashing some people, especially the Hillary Clinton die-hards. Alternatively, those Democrats are just happy to have the media tarnishing Donald Trump's name.

Whatever the case, it has not stopped respected world leaders from associating with the US president. To emphasize the extremity of the media bias, Tony Blair cited instances when the media has compared Donald Trump to dictators Joseph Stalin of the former Soviet Union, and Adolf Hitler of Nazi Germany. With such unwarranted comparisons, nobody needs convincing that the media is just hateful of Trump.

Israeli Prime Minister, Benjamin Netanyahu, was delighted to meet with President Trump despite the bad press the US president has been receiving. Even his wife and Trump's wife, Melania, had something about the presidency to talk about. Without doubt, Prime Minister Netanyahu would like the US to have a president who supports Israel and its political stance in world matters, and more so in the Middle East, and he sees such a person in Trump. He, obviously, cannot understand why the US media is so much against the president, when he is upholding policies such as the US being an ally of Israel, which has been long standing with successive US regimes.

As wives of the two leaders spoke after the Trumps landed in Israel, Melania Trump pointed out to Sara Netanyahu that the media back home did not like the Trumps, to which Mrs. Netanyahu responded that it was the same with them in Israel. Trump and Netanyahu concurred. However, Mrs. Netanyahu was quick to add that the people of Israel liked the Prime Minister and his family, and they liked the Trumps because the Netanyahus spoke well of them. Such interactions serve to confirm that media propaganda has not succeeded in turning world leaders against President Trump, and that the president is not about to succumb to media pressure, but is steadfast in pursuing the goals his administration has set.

Chapter 7:

Scholars Vindicate Media Critics

When patriotic citizens allege undue criticism of Donald Trump by the media, Hillary die-hards think that is blind support for the president from Trump fanatics. Gladly, facts are coming up every other day to confirm it is true that media has been treating President Trump unfairly in their reporting. As has been pointed out, Trump is relating well with world leaders, and his meeting with Israeli Prime Minister is just one example.

Harvard Study Confirms Negative Coverage

The few journalists who have been objective in their reporting of matters related to Donald Trump, and those who have criticized their colleagues' prejudicial reporting of Trump, have either been frowned upon or discreetly mocked. Some media personalities who are die-hard Hillary Clinton supporters cannot help rolling their eyes on live TV when someone mentions how prejudiced the media is against Trump. They know it is true they dislike Trump and enjoy reporting the worst of him, but they would not admit it. This goes to show that non-acceptance of Donald Trump as a worthy leader is not purely political or intellectual, but personal. Some journalists simply despise Trump because he beat their favorite candidate, Hillary Clinton, and nothing else.

Fortunately, after watching the media and realizing it is saturated with negative reporting about Trump as a person and also as president, some scholars have decided to embark on surveys, to ascertain how objective or subjective the US media has been in matters relating to President Trump. What the group of scholars at the prestigious Harvard University has discovered has vindicated everyone who has been saying the media is depriving Donald Trump of his due credit. The media critics have been proven right in alleging that media is unduly tarnishing the name of Donald Trump and his presidency.

The study, which was conducted at the Shorenstein Center on Media, Politics and Public Policy at Harvard University, showed that although both President's George W. Bush and Bill Clinton received negative coverage during their first 100 days of their presidency, Trump's negative coverage has gone overboard. For the two former presidents, the ratio of negative coverage versus positive coverage was 60% to 40%, whereas that of President Trump during a similar period was 80% to 20%. It is easy to trust this report, not just because it comes from a scholarly report from a credible institution, but also because Harvard has not been known to particularly like conservative ideas and their proponents.

Such negative publicity, in content and in tone, cannot be assumed to be normal for a new president. For one, the publicity Bush and Clinton received from the media, as seen from their percentages, was only a little bit skewed towards the negative, whereas that of President Trump is drastically inclined towards the negative; actually moving close to blatant condemnation of the president. This shows that a big section of the media is being vindictive of Donald Trump, and setting aside thoughts and decisions that would be good for the country.

It seems that the US media enjoys playing kingmaker. When it tried to hype up everyone to see the goodness of electing Hillary Clinton, it chose to close its eyes to Hillary Clinton's weaknesses as seen during her long political career. Now that she lost the election despite the massive support from the media, they are trying to bash President Trump and digging dirt, probably with the hope he might be impeached. There is a big contrast between the way the media is treating Trump and the way they treated President Barack Obama when he first became US President. They gave him so much goodwill that his ratings in the first 100 days of his presidency were very high – 65% as compared to Trump's 41%. Obama's media coverage was 60% positive against just 40% that was negative.

Fox news ran a study on August 24, 2017 depicting the percentage of negative news coverage that President Trump receives from various news sources and concluded the following: CNN's negative coverage 93%, NBC 93%, CBS 91%, NYT 87%, WAPO 83%, and WS 70%. What a shame!

Mainstream Media is the Worst

Although President Trump's negative portrayal by the media is very high at 80%, it is even worse when it comes to individual mainstream media houses. The Harvard study showed that the negative coverage the president has been receiving from CNN as well as NBC is as high as 93%, while that from CBS goes as high as 91%. This means the media houses have found extremely little good to report about President Trump. Those who dispute the allegations that mainstream media are against Donald Trump often cite Fox News, which was seen to highlight Trump's strengths during the 2016 presidential campaigns. Nevertheless, the Harvard study has shown that even Fox News has not been exactly fair to the president. During his first 100 days in office, Fox News gave President Trump 52% negative coverage. That is not something you would expect of a friendly or objective media house.

Media Ignored Clinton's Scandals

If the media had been objective with Trump, probably Trump's supporters would not notice the silence surrounding Hillary Clinton's scandals. The media downplayed the significance of bad behavior linked to Hillary Clinton's allies as well as Hillary Clinton's poor judgment. For example, the leaks about the Democratic National Committee conspiring against other politicians, and the disclosure that some journalists were providing Hillary Clinton with presidential debate information in advance were serious enough to scandalize her presidency.

Yet the media made it a non-issue and proceeded to focus on scandalizing Trump. Any objective person could see that the media was unabashedly pro-Clinton and blatantly anti-Trump. Going by such clear examples, it is difficult to tell when the media is telling the truth about President Trump and when it is just playing Democratic Party puppet.

Chapter 8:

Trump's Low Approval Ratings Are Meaningless

Normally, low approval ratings for the president would mean that Americans do not like the president or do not approve of what he is doing. However, for President Trump, it needs to be looked at alongside the poor ratings he received as he competed against Hillary Clinton. In July 2017, mainstream media reported that the president's rating was a paltry 36%, which was worse than that of Gerald Ford back in 1975 – 39%. US presidents generally have higher ratings during their first year in office, and this low rating by Trump would ordinarily be worrying to Americans. However, the US populace has gotten used to the media giving Donald Trump bad press, and knowing how influential the media can be when it comes to people's perceptions, they are not particularly shocked.

One reason that makes objective Americans not believe the ratings is the source. This particular poll that puts President Trump among the most poorly rated US president in history was conducted by *ABC News* and the *Washington Post*, two media organizations that have consistently manifested anti-Trump tendencies.

Low Ratings During Campaigns Were A Sham

Another reason is the fact that if ratings were that significant in Trump's case, he would not have won the US presidency considering the low ratings he was given against Hillary Clinton. All the way from mid-2015 to almost the end of 2016, major media players gave Hillary Clinton a clear lead, indicating to the general public that she was the president US citizens wanted. Even with all that media bias, Donald Trump defeated Hillary Clinton to become the 45th president of the United States. Using that scenario as a parallel, it is alright to dismiss the current low ratings given to Trump and call them meaningless.

Experts Say the Economy Is Doing Well

It is easy to understand a president's low ratings when the country's economy is on a nosedive, but in Trump's case, the economy is doing well and has been consistently doing so. Even better is the prediction by experts that the growth rate for Growth Domestic Product (GDP) is likely to remain at the ideal range of between 2% and 3%. As far as the experts are concerned, the country is not exposed to either too much inflation or too much deflation. Needless to say, if the country's leadership was questionable and unpredictable as the media likes to portray Trump, the US economy would not have been this stable, let alone growing. In fact, an objective person evaluating such positive factors as the economy would not give the media ratings of the US president a second look.

Even CNN, one of the media houses that have been emphasizing President Trump's low ratings, has reported how well the country's economy has been doing. They say the country has benefitted from creation of a million more jobs since Trump became president, not counting another 209,000 that the economy gained in July 2017 alone. CNN Money also reported that unemployment, which has remained at 10% since 2009, has dropped to a bearable 4.3%. One wonders what other indicators media expects to see before they can report positively about President Trump.

Many economists say the United States is at or near "full employment," meaning the unemployment rate won't go down significantly more. Unemployment is down and new jobs are being created.

Unfortunately, instead of reporting on the positive gains and giving hope to Americans, the media quickly puts aside Donald Trump's positives, and begins to dig up the scandalous bits of old news – like Trump's administration's link to Russia! How sad. How so very sad.

Chapter 9:

Trump's Win Against the Fake Media

The fake Media's war against President Trump seems endless, even as it is, for the most part, baseless. Unfortunately, such antagonism is not good for the US even if President Trump has found a way to weather the storm. When the media reports as if the president is just about to be indicted, there is the danger of risk-averse investors putting a pause to any arrangements they were making to invest in the US. Ordinarily, even some local investors might be tempted to take some of their investments out of the US, under a veil of diversification.

Luckily, many serious investors engage with individuals on the ground as part of their due diligence, to get the real picture of what Trump's media image is doing to life in the US. Granted the fake news can be annoying to anyone, and it sure irritates Donald Trump at times. This is, very likely, the reason the president uses social media platforms, mainly twitter, to discredit any rumors about him, or to poke holes on fake stories broadcast by the media. While President Trump could be risking displaying his strong emotions on an issue, as opposed to waiting to address it diplomatically, his head-on approach seems to have worked in his favor so far.

The tweeting he used to do during the presidential campaigns has become a constant undertaking. Trump has been putting his rebuttal against fake news by the media through the internet. Not only is this a blow to the mainstream media that attracts viewership when discussing directly with a prominent person, but it is also an effective method of clarifying issues about Trump's administration that the media deliberately misrepresents. No wonder the public has not raised dust over the fake allegations the media has been making against President Trump and members of his administration.

In fact, Trump has rubbed mainstream media the wrong way by bragging that he is a hero to his followers whose total exceed 30 million. According to Byron York, one of Washington Post's columnists, Donald Trump is happy to engage his opponents on social media, and he is certain to emerge the victor in the eyes of his followers. Clearly, the president is not cowed by the fake media, and instead, revels in tearing down their fake allegations and exposing the malicious reporting for what it is. For example, in August 2017, President Trump tweeted, "hard to believe that with 24/7 false news on CNN, ABC, NBC, CBS, NYT, and WAPO the Trump base is getting stronger."

Economy Growing Despite Fake News

The US public is not left to wonder at any one time what their president's stance on a hot issue is, and that is because of his regular communication on social media. This habit is likely to have kept his White House staff on their toes, because there is no way the president would tolerate being behind his staff with regard to information on pertinent issues. Such a situation can only serve to decrease efficiency among the staff. There are different dimensions to this president-public interaction, some very beneficial.

For one, whenever Trump contradicts the media, the public is provoked into reasoning. Individuals who would otherwise have taken the media reporting at face value embark on seeking facts from independent sources, and at the end of the day they can tell when the news is fake or outright malicious. Some people even think the president should not accept to give interviews to mainstream media because of the media's outright bias, but he does not seem to care. After all, by accepting to be interviewed by the same people who spread falsehoods about him, he sends a clear message to the millions of American masses that he has nothing to hide, and that he has good reason for taking every action he has taken as their president.

US Masses Have Confidence in Trump

Clearly, Trump has managed to retain the confidence of the masses. If he had not, there would be a red flag in the US stock market. Individuals would have dashed to offload their shares fearing a slump, and companies would have followed suit. Obviously, such an eventuality would have led to a dip in stock prices. Although some Democrats and mainstream media push to keep the Russia scandal alive, and claim that Trump is a white supremacists, and claim that he has dementia or a mental defect, and other negative untrue media reports and statements; the stock market is thriving and experts are predicting continued good performance in the coming months. The stock market has reached some of its highest highs in decades.

This should surprise the media and make them change tune, but it seems like they are too blinded by their prejudice and personal hatred against President Trump. The same media that has continued to portray Trump as being bad for the US is the same one reporting the facts of a thriving economy. It should be a wake-up call for them, but apparently this is not happening. Nevertheless, Trump's win against the fake media is coming gradually in the form of America's progress. As more and more US citizens get employment and stop relying on government welfare, and as people's investments continue to grow in value, they are going to realize that Trump is a man of his word.

Better still, when people continue to see more and more meetings between President Trump and other world leaders, they are going to realize that Trump is not going to lead the US into isolation as Hillary Clinton and her sycophant media friends have always tried to portray. With time, people in the US, citizens and foreign investors alike, are going to take everything the media reports about Trump with a pinch of salt. Hopefully, when the fake news becomes redundant, media houses might develop new policies that encourage truth and objectivity. In the meantime, the general public will continue to listen to President Trump's voice on YouTube and learn his version of important events from his tweets, and the rest of his successes will manifest itself through people's improving quality of life. According to USA today the stock-market has hit all-time highs. The morale and the optimism of the American people is good.

CONCLUSION ONE

I hope this book has opened your eyes to things that are very important in this life, and in America. And that is, if we really want the blessings of GOD, peace, and harmony in a society; we must always support the truth and people who are standing for the truth and who are trying to uplift humanity. I am very aware that we ALL have our own specific truth; however, there is a resounding truth that is innately encoded in ALL of us individually as American citizens; that we cannot deny. That TRUTH is hard-wired into ALL of our individual psyches and subconsciousness and we hear that voice from birth. So, let us yield to it when necessary.

Further, never listen to one side of a story. Do not get involved with hearsay, he-say, or she-say. Do not immediately jump to conclusions. Do not let a media soundbite force you to draw a negative conclusion about someone or convict them. Listen to both sides of the story and gather all the evidence and information before drawing a conclusion or convicting. This is basic moral law and basic human decency. It is virtually impossible for us to know everything about the many things that are going on in this world; only GOD can do that. Therefore, if you cannot or do not have time to get both sides of the story, leave it alone and do not convict or draw a conclusion because it is not fair. Be a big enough MAN or a big enough WOMAN to say "I do not know all the facts and circumstances; or I do not know the whole story, and thus, I really cannot honestly and accurately comment." It's just that simple. Don't be a punk, a chump, a peon, or sissified; and try to comment or condemn situations you do not have all the facts about!!!

And also, know this, if you always look for something wrong in a person, you will always find it. Because not one of us is perfect. But most importantly, when YOU treat someone wrongfully, remember what YOU did to others, when people prejudge you without due process; when your time comes. Because if you treat people in the wrongful manner above, it will surely come back your way some day. It is easy to be lazy, judgmental, unfair, unlawful, a liar, and/or un-caring. But, there are no rewards for this, rather, there is downfall.

Always play by the rules and by the law. Or if you wish, and you don't think the law is fair and just, work through your legislature to get the law changed, if possible. But, we must have laws and rules that people obey to live in harmony and to have a successful nation. That is why I like Trump. He will enforce the laws and rules; and Trump is consistent.

We have a Beautiful country called "AMERICA," let us protect its ideals at all cost!

CONCLUSION TWO

It should be obvious at the end of this book that we have some serious issues in America to confront. We have a much divided nation at this point in our journey together. There are some Democrats not playing by the rules; there are some Republicans not playing by the rules; there are some Black Americans playing the race-card and screaming racism every chance they get; there are anti-Trump protesters breaking the law during their protests; and the saddest part is that the FAKE main stream media is trying to politically destroy a man based on lies and false premises; and they will not report accurate news. This is probably the biggest problem right now, the "FAKE MEDIA."

This cannot and will not be tolerated and the true righteous Americans, such as ourselves, must rise up every chance we get and fight against it within the confines of the law until this evil tide is dissipated. The fake media has become a very destructive force in our society; not just in politics, but in all facets of American life. The FAKE media must be pushed back in its place.

I am optimistic and know this will be done. How do I know? I know because the majority of us as Americans (Black, white, brown, and others) had the ability to see that Donald John Trump was the best candidate for president, out of the two candidates; even though we were bombarded constantly by falsehoods and untruths by the fake media and the Clinton ads machine, daily.

However, make no mistake, we must continue to fight and seek the truth, because if we do not, we will cause America to become a place that has no favor with GOD.

I wrote this book because I want to expose people and entities who have allowed themselves to be overcome and consumed by HATRED; JEAOLOUSY; UNTRUTH; IMMATURITY; EXTREME BIAS; BLACK RACISM; WHITE RACISM; RACISM; UNFAIRNESS; and CONSPIRACY to distort the truth and goodwill. Also, to expose those who no longer seek the truth; nor follow the rules; or the law. If you are consumed with the negative ills above, please remove yourself, or get out of the way of True Americans! We will not tolerate your behavior!

Again, these people should be penalized or marginalized (depending on the circumstances) until they have come back to their senses. True Americans will carry you or tolerate you until you come back to your senses, but you cannot stand in the way of American progress. We cannot let you do that. America is not the place to allow hatred and bigotry to abide or to be at the forefront of our American Culture. We have come too far for that.

This speaks for Blacks, Whites, Browns, Yellows, and all other people who make up America. I myself, as a Black-American, will continue to support all that is good in this country so we can continue to grow toward the graces and good favor of GOD.

I must also ad, that there are some good sincere people that are opposed to Trump and have some very valid reasons, concerns, and positions. I also know that some people are really sincerely concerned about the country and want to see it do well and oppose President Trump for these very reasons. I also know that some who sincerely oppose President Trump do so based upon what they "think" is true from the fake media.--I do not fight against people who sincerely believe that they are standing for the right cause or supporting the best person. All of these people are not to blame. We all have the right to believe and support what we wish and what we feel is right; as long as we play by the rules and follow the law.

However, there IS a great political divide in our Country and it really baffles me to see the opposing side fashion their beliefs based on the current facts. Most of the time, I really do not understand the other sides logic and rational. But, I have also noticed, that the other side, in the same vain, does not understand my logic and rational of why I continue to support and believe in Donald Trump.

This has become really baffling to me. Yet, I have noticed that people on the opposing side are baffled by my positions as well, as a supporter of Donald Trump. And thus, we have a great divide in America consisting of two opposing sides that are really baffled by the other side's views and beliefs. Nevertheless, and yet again, I can deal with that, as long as the opposing side, but really both sides, continues to play by the rules and follow the laws.

BUT, it is those who know the truth and turn a blind eye; those who create lies and untruths; those who do not follow the law or the rules; those who are filled with hatred and jealousy; those who have personal motives and hate President Trump on a personal level; those who do not have the country as their greatest concern in mind; and most importantly, the FAKE MEDIA who is the greatest purveyor of ill-will and discord for our country. These are the people and entities who need to be penalized and/or marginalized and/or expelled from our society if they do not wish to change!!!

THE SOLUTION TO THE DILEMMA

With our country in such a great divide; and with both sides having very strong emotions, feelings, beliefs, and convictions for their particular party or principals; we are at each other's throats as never before in America. Neither side is necessarily totally wrong; nor is neither side necessarily totally right. We are ALL good Americans; and we ALL have some very strong convictions and beliefs. So, we need to try to mend this divide!

Therefore, there has to be a median by which we can come to some common resolves and solutions to nullify or dilute this divide; which is not healthy for our Nation and is not the will of GOD. GOD does not intend for us to be at a great divide in America. And thus, we must apply basic biblical principles and basic moral contentiousness to this problem.

There is a solution, and if both sides and all Americans would apply it to this great political divide, and apply it to their daily living, this great divide will dissipate or at the least be majorly reduced or diluted. We are a great people! We are great Americans! And we can do much better than this! And we must do better than this!

If Americans will follow the following advice and instructions, this will solve, or majorly dilute the dilemma; and it is quite simple. Some may not take it serious or may not see the major and profound effects it can and will have to resolve this problem; but if we all apply it, it can and will.

If Americans will start to do the following, our problems would be solved or greatly depreciated; and again it is quite simple: The only thing that will mend us back together as American people is for us to start to play by the rules, by the laws, and by basic biblical principles.

Well, what does that mean, you may ask. To put it in one sentence, it simply means this: **PEOPLE IN AMERICA NEED TO START TO PLAY BY THE LEGAL RULES, THE LEGAL LAWS, THE MORAL RULES, THE MORAL LAWS, THE ETHICAL RULES, AND THE ETHICAL LAWS.** It's just that simple. **ALL OF THESE RULES AND LAWS ENCOMPASS BASIC BIBLICAL PRINCIPLES, WHICH WHEN APPLIED, HARMONY ABOUNDS AND PEOPLE GET ALONG AND LIVE IN PEACE.**

As I explained earlier in this book, we ALL have a conscience and innately know right from wrong and justice vs. injustice. Further, all of our legal laws, our moral laws, our ethical laws, and our US Constitution stem directly from basic biblical principles. If we all sincerely and fairly apply these basic principles in our Politics and in our daily personal lives, these problems will be resolved. End of story.

So I say! Thank GOD for GOOD Black people, thank God for GOOD White people, thank GOD for GOOD Brown people, thank GOD for GOOD Yellow people, and thank GOD for ALL GOOD people.

THE AMERICAN PEOPLE ARE THE MOST RESEILIENT PEOPLE ON THE EARTH!!! SO LET'S APPLY THESE SIMPLE BASIC PRINCIPLES AND KEEP IT THAT WAY!!!

CONTINUE TO NEXT PAGE FOR THE GOOD NEWS ...

CONCLUSION THREE
"THE GOOD NEWS"

One good thing that has come from this recent era of political division that many may not have noticed is: Although we are a very politically divided Country in regards to politics and along the political spectrum at this time in our American History, we are not as divided along White and Black racist color lines as much as we have been in the past. Our political differences have expanded a great deal beyond racism along Black and White color lines; our political differences "now" are along the lines of deep-seeded political beliefs that we hold dear. This is a sign that we as Black and White Americans are growing and have truly grown closer together as a people. This is a very good thing!!!

BUT again, the ultimate good news is that the majority of Americans, Black, White, Brown and Yellow are wise enough to see through the lies of the fake media and others; and are able to come together when needed and support "GOOD" to uplift this country. THIS DEFINITELY MEANS THAT THE MAJORITY OF AMERICANS ARE RIGHTEOUS PEOPLE AND WANT TO SEE THE TRUTH PREVAIL IN THIS COUNTRY. FANTASTIC!!

Therefore I conclude:

SHOULD TRUMP WIN AGAINST THE FAKE MEDIA? YES!!!

WHY? Because I truly feel that Donald Trump believes he is doing what he thinks is in the best interest of America and what GOD wants him to do.

WILL TRUMP WIN AGAINST THE FAKE MEDIA? YES!!!

WHY? Because when a person is striving to do good and what they feel is right within their own heart, there is no stopping the "drive" of that person to do what they feel is right.

DOES THE FAKE MEDIA CARE ABOUT THE TRUTH ANYMORE?

IT SEEMS AS THOUGH THEY DO NOT. NEVERTHELESS, THROUGH OUR OWN EFFORTS, WE AS CONCERNED AMERICANS MUST BRING THE FAKE MEDIA BACK AROUND TO BEING WHAT IT IS SUPPOSE TO BE; OR DISPEL THEM.

Finally, if you don't have anything positive or at least fair to offer, PLEASE, get out of President Trump's way and let him do what is in his heart to do. As Americans, we need consistency in the Presidency. In President Donald John Trump, there is true consistency and true sincere convictions. President Trump has "MUCH" to offer America. America needs a face-lift; a rehab; and a full complete overhaul. President Trump is about to give us that. Let him work his magic!!!

President Trump is EAGER to make America great again, he is EAGER to do good things for the American people, and he is EAGER to do what he feels is GOD'S work through him. I firmly believe that President Trump is about to bring America to a major "APEX." And I also truly believe President Trump is going to create a greater "NEW MODEL" for the office of the Presidency. Believe me!!!

Thank you for reading this book. I hope you enjoyed it and learned something from it. Please share with a friend or family member. May GOD bless you and keep "you" and your "spirit" safe. **Dr. Zeke**

References

1) Voters See More Anti-Trump, Pro-Hillary Bias in Media

   http://www.rasmussenreports.com/public_content/politi cs/elections/election_2016/voters_see_more_anti_trum p_pro_hillary_bias_in_media

2) Mainstream media maligned: 10 examples of blatant bias

   http://www.washingtontimes.com/news/2016/nov/8/mai nstream-media-maligned-10-examples-blatant-bias/

3) NBC News not even trying to hide its Hillary bias

   http://nypost.com/2016/10/18/nbc-news-not-even-trying-to-hide-its-hillary-bias/

4) Conservative Christians pan 'prosperity gospel' Trump inaugural preacher

   http://www.washingtonexaminer.com/conservative-christians-pan-prosperity-gospel-trump-inaugural-preacher/article/2610564

5) Trump sacking Corey Lewandowski:

   https://www.nytimes.com/2016/06/21/us/politics/corey-lewandowski-donald-trump.html

6) U.S. submits formal notice of withdrawal from Paris climate pact

   https://www.reuters.com/article/us-un-climate-usa-paris-idUSKBN1AK2FM

7) All False statements involving Hillary Clinton

http://www.politifact.com/personalities/hillary-clinton/statements/byruling/false/

8) Clinton wrongly says FBI director sent letter about emails 'only' to Republicans

http://*www*.politifact.com/truth-o-meter/statements/2016/oct/30/hillary-clinton/clinton-wrongly-says-fbi-director-sent-letter-abou/

9) How Hillary Lied to Parents of Benghazi Dead

www.nationalreview.com/article/438657/hillary-clintons-benghazi-lies-pat-*smith*-charles-woods

10) The Benghazi Timeline, Clinton Edition

http://www.factcheck.org/2016/06/the-benghazi-timeline-clinton-edition/

11) Sanders freshly questions Clinton's 'judgment' in video

http://*www*.politico.com/story/2016/06/bernie-sanders-clinton-judgement-223874

12) Ex-Secret Service agent: Hillary Clinton 'occasionally violent'

http://*thehill.com/blogs/in-the-know/in-the-know/282330-ex-secret-service-agent-clinton-occasionally-violent*

13) Ex-Secret Service agent: Hillary Clinton 'occasionally violent'

http://*thehill.com/blogs/in-the-know/in-the-know/282330-ex-secret-service-agent-clinton-occasionally-violent*

14) Blacks have reason for optimism with Trump this Black History Month

Ref: http://thehill.com/blogs/pundits-blog/civil-rights/317635-blacks-have-reason-for-optimism-with-trump-this-black-history

15) Democrats love bashing Trump. But that alone won't help them win again

   https*://www.theguardian.com/commentisfree/2017/jun/23/democrats-love-bashing-trump-wont-help-win*

16) The Media's Unhealthy Trump-Russia Obsession ... By The Numbers

   http://www.investors.com/politics/editorials/the-medias-unhealthy-trump-russia-obsession-by-the-numbers/

17) 5 facts about illegal immigration in the U.S.

   http: //www.pewresearch.org/fact-tank/

18) Trump: 'No politician in history has been treated more unfairly'

   https://www.theguardian.com/us-news/2017/may/17/donald-trump-presidency-media-coverage-russia-scandal

19) Tony Blair says 'left media' is being unfair on Donald Trump

   http://www.plive.co.ke/bi/politics/politics-tony-blair-says-left-media-is-being-unfair-on-donald-trump-id6665292.html

20) Harvard study: Media has been largely negative on Trump

http://www.chicagotribune.com/news/columnists/kass/ct-trump-media-coverage-harvard-kass-0521-20170519-column.html

21) Presidential Job Approval Ratings Following the First 100 Days

http://www.presidency.ucsb.edu/data/100days_approval.php

22) Poll: Trump's six-month approval rating hits historic low

http://www.politico.com/story/2017/07/16/trump-approval-rating-historic-low-240598

23) Poll: Trump's six-month approval rating hits historic low

http://elections.huffingtonpost.com/pollster/2016-general-election-trump-vs-clinton

24) US Economic Outlook: For 2017 and Beyond

https://www.thebalance.com/us-economic-outlook-3305669

25) Over half of modern presidents never hit an approval rating as low as Trump

http://edition.cnn.com/2017/07/18/politics/trump-low-approval-compare/index.html

26) Milestone for Trump: 1 million new jobs in six months

http://money.cnn.com/2017/08/04/news/economy/july-jobs-report/index.html

27) Democrats Renew Push to Probe Deutsche Bank Russia Scandal

https://www.bloomberg.com/news/articles/2017-08-11/house-democrats-renew-push-to-force-probe-of-deutsche-bank

28) Why July may have set up the stock market for a very good year

https://www.cnbc.com/2017/07/31/why-july-may-have-set-up-the-stock-market-for-a-very-good-year.html

29) How the economy is really doing

http://money.cnn.com/2017/05/05/investing/trump-economy-report-card-jobs/index.html

30) How Dangerous Is President Trump's 'Fake News' Rhetoric?

http://www.huffingtonpost.com/entry/how-dangerous-is-president-trumps-fake-news-rhetoric_us_5973a737e4b0545a5c310094

31) Trump wins the media war, battle by battle

http://www.washingtontimes.com/news/2017/jul/2/inside-the-beltway-trump-wins-the-media-war-battle/

www.ingramcontent.com/pod-product-compliance
Lightning Source LLC
Chambersburg PA
CBHW062118280526
45787CB00009B/873